DEDICATION

To the children who will lead with love.

Send Inquiries to:
BannonRiverBooks@gmail.com

For More by the Author:
www.ColleenBrunetti.com

Share a Little Kindness

Written and Illustrated By

Colleen Brunetti

Share a little
kindness, Love.
Be the good
that others see.

Look inside and
you will find
everything that
you can be.

Give without a
second thought.
Always give to
those in need.

For when you share
all that you have,
you plant a perfect
little seed.

Try your best
with all your might.
Even try when
you are down.

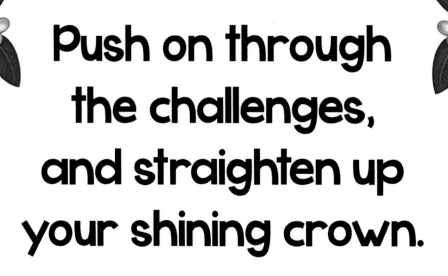

Push on through
the challenges,
and straighten up
your shining crown.

Choose your words
so carefully,
even if you
feel offended.

Gentle words can
calm the storm.
And friendships
surely can be mended.

Always say you're sorry
when you know that
you've done
something wrong.

And, "It's okay,
I will forgive,"
can sometimes be
the sweetest song.

Spend some time
in nature, Love.
Take a breath in
slow and deep.

Listen to the
wind and waves
as they sing
you off to sleep.

Run and jump
and play today.
Go outside,
be wild and free.

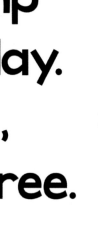

Imagining will take
you far.
You never know
what you can be.

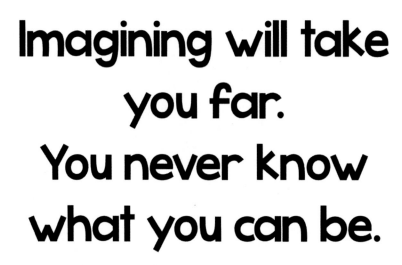

Go and read
a story, Love.
Books are magic,
yes, it's true.

A book can take
you anywhere,
and the journey's
up to you.

Listen close
when others speak.
Give to them
your kindest ear.

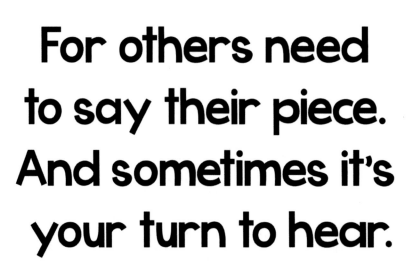

For others need
to say their piece.
And sometimes it's
your turn to hear.

You have the right
to say, "Please stop!"
Or, "I don't like
the things you do."

Be strong and brave
and speak your truth.
Because you are
in charge of you.

Always find
the magic, Love.
Always look out
for the light.

Even in the
darkness, Love,
be sure to keep
it in your sight.

Every day's a
new beginning.
Every day you
have a choice.

You can make
a difference.
Just be BOLD
and raise your lovely voice!

This book is full of special things from all over the world!
Did you know...

There are 19 species of owls in North America.

The largest butterflies in the world can be found in Australia.

Sloths of South America spend most of their time upside down.

Europe is home to amazing architecture... and French bulldogs!

The Southern Lights are visible from Antarctica, being watched here by emporer penguins.

Giraffes in Africa are the tallest land animals in the world.

Found in Asia, groups of peacocks are called parties.

Friends can be found all over the world! Our differences make us special, our kindness to one another makes us one.

MEET COLLEEN

Colleen Brunetti grew up in the rolling green hills of Vermont, where she spent much of her time devouring books. That love of literacy led to a career as a teacher, and later an author. Today she spends her time with her husband, chasing their two kids and various fur balls, and dreaming up future publications. This is her third children's book.

"Share a Little Kindness"
is Colleen's first self- illustrated project.

Visit www.ColleenBrunetti.com
to purchase books, art prints,
and get free downloads!

Made in the USA
Monee, IL
11 December 2023

48900004R00019